D1710173

World of Mammals

Kangaroos

by Xavier Niz

Consultant:
Suzanne B. McLaren
Collection Manager, Section of Mammals
Carnegie Museum of Natural History
Edward O'Neil Research Center
Pittsburgh, Pennsylvania

Capstone press
Mankato, Minnesota

Bridgestone Books are published by Capstone Press,
151 Good Counsel Drive, P.O. Box 669, Mankato, Minnesota 56002.
www.capstonepress.com

Library of Congress Cataloging-in-Publication Data
Niz, Xavier.
    Kangaroos / by Xavier Niz.
    p. cm.—(Bridgestone Books. World of mammals)
    Includes bibliographical references and index.
    ISBN-13: 978-0-7368-3719-4 (hardcover)
    ISBN-10: 0-7368-3719-1 (hardcover)
    1. Kangaroos—Juvenile literature. I. Title. II. Series: World of mammals.
QL737.M35N59 2005
599.2'22—dc22   2004015345

Summary: A brief introduction to kangaroos, discussing their characteristics, habitat, life cycle,
    and predators. Includes a range map, life cycle illustration, and amazing facts.

Editorial Credits
Erika L. Shores, editor; Molly Nei, set designer; Ted Williams, book designer; Erin Scott, Wylde Hare
    Creative, illustrator; Kelly Garvin, photo researcher; Scott Thoms, photo editor

Photo Credits
Bruce Coleman Inc./J&D Bartlett, 10
Digital Vision/NatPhotos, 1, 20
James P. Rowan, 12
Minden Pictures/Mitsuaki Iwago, 18
Nature Picture Library/Staffan Widstrand, cover
Tom Stack & Associates, Inc./Dave Watts, 4, 6, 16

1 2 3 4 5 6 10 09 08 07 06 05

Table of Contents

Kangaroos

Kangaroos are animals that hop on two strong back legs. Female kangaroos carry their young in a pouch on their stomach. Kangaroos can be taller than a person or smaller than a cat.

Kangaroos are **marsupials**. Marsupials are **mammals** that carry their young in pouches. Marsupials, like all mammals, are **warm-blooded** and have backbones. Opossums and koalas are also marsupials.

◄ A young kangaroo rides in its mother's pouch.

What Kangaroos Look Like

All kinds of kangaroos have similar body parts. Kangaroos have small heads with big ears. They have short front legs. Kangaroos hop on two large back legs. They use their muscular tails to balance.

Male kangaroos are usually bigger than female kangaroos. The largest kangaroo is the male red kangaroo. It grows as large as 6.5 feet (2 meters) tall. The smallest kangaroos are rat kangaroos. Rat kangaroos only grow to be about 21 inches (53 centimeters) tall.

◀ Kangaroos have faces that look like deer.

Kangaroos Range Map

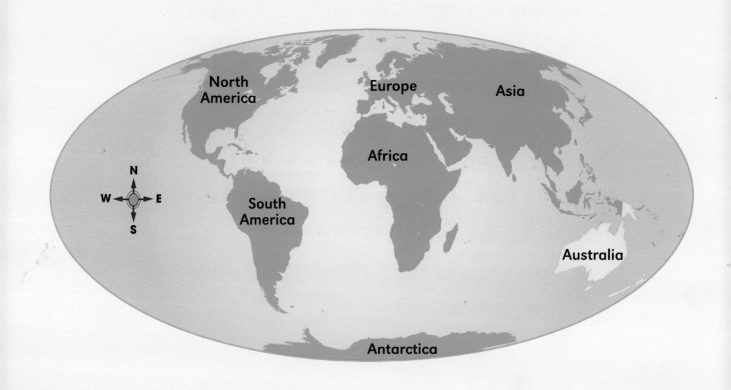

Where Kangaroos Live

Kangaroos in the World

Kangaroos live in Australia, Papua New Guinea, and a few nearby islands. Australia has the most kangaroos.

Eastern gray kangaroos live in eastern Australia. People often see them because they live near Australia's largest cities.

Red kangaroos are not seen as often. They live in the center of Australia where few people live.

◄ Australia is home to the most kangaroos.

Kangaroo Habitats

Kangaroos live in many **habitats**. Red kangaroos live in deserts and dry grasslands. Gray kangaroos live in forests and grasslands.

The weather is hot where most kangaroos live. Kangaroos rest in the shade during the day. They look for food at night when it's cooler.

◄ Kangaroos hop through the forests where they live.

What Kangaroos Eat

Most kangaroos eat only plants. Kangaroos eat plants and grasses that grow in their habitats. Some small kangaroos also eat insects and worms.

Kangaroos need very little water to survive. Kangaroos can live for months without drinking any water. Kangaroos save water in their bodies by resting during the daytime.

◄ Kangaroos chew flowers and leaves off of plants.

The Life Cycle of a Kangaroo

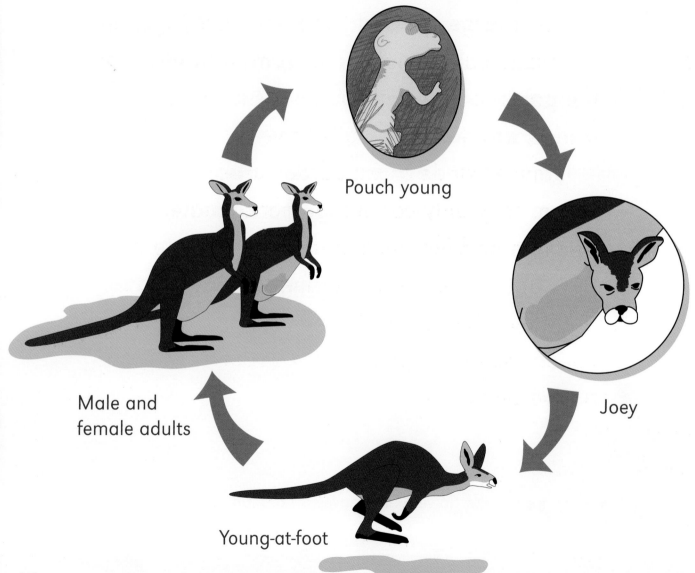

Pouch young

Joey

Young-at-foot

Male and female adults

14

Producing Young

Most large kinds of kangaroos live together in groups called mobs. The **dominant** male in the group is called a boomer. The boomer **mates** with females, called flyers.

Smaller kinds of kangaroos usually live alone. They only come together to mate.

Male and female kangaroos can mate any time of the year. About a month after mating, a female gives birth. The tiny offspring is called the pouch young. It is about as big as a lima bean.

Growing Up

After it is born, the pouch young crawls into its mother's pouch. It drinks milk from its mother. The pouch young soon grows fur on its body.

Six months after birth, the pouch young can leave the pouch. It is then called a joey. The joey stays with its mother for about a year. When the joey grows too large for the pouch, it is called a young-at-foot. After two years, the young-at-foot is an adult.

◄ Young kangaroos stay close to their mothers.

Dangers to Kangaroos

Many animals hunt kangaroos. Eagles, pythons, and large lizards kill joeys and old kangaroos. Wild dogs called dingoes hunt large kangaroos. People hunt kangaroos for their meat and hides. Some sheep ranchers think kangaroos are pests. Kangaroos sometimes eat food left out for sheep.

People have built national parks to protect kangaroos. Kangaroos are safe from hunters in these areas. Many people want kangaroos to survive in the wild.

◄ People put up fences to keep kangaroos off their land.

Amazing Facts about Kangaroos

- Male kangaroos sometimes fight. They box each other with their front legs. They also kick each other with their hind legs.
- A large kangaroo can hop as fast as 30 miles (48 kilometers) per hour.
- Kangaroos usually live about six to eight years.
- Kangaroos take a spit bath to stay cool. They lick their front legs to cool off. Just like dogs, kangaroos also pant to keep cool.

◄ Male kangaroos fight to decide who gets to mate with a female kangaroo.

Glossary

dominant (DOM-uh-nuhnt)—the most powerful member of a group

habitat (HAB-uh-tat)—the place and natural conditions in which an animal lives

mammal (MAM-uhl)—a warm-blooded animal that has a backbone; female mammals feed milk to their young.

marsupial (mar-SOO-pee-uhl)—an animal that carries its young in a pouch

mate (MAYT)—to join together to produce young

warm-blooded (warm-BLUHD-id)—having a body temperature that stays the same

Read More

Murray, Julie. *Kangaroos.* Animal Kingdom. Edina, Minn.: Abdo, 2003.

Noonan, Diana. *The Kangaroo.* Life Cycles. Philadelphia: Chelsea Clubhouse Books, 2003.

Internet Sites

FactHound offers a safe, fun way to find Internet sites related to this book. All of the sites on FactHound have been researched by our staff.

Here's how:
1. Visit *www.facthound.com*
2. Type in this special code **0736837191** for age-appropriate sites. Or enter a search word related to this book for a more general search.
3. Click on the **Fetch It** button.

FactHound will fetch the best sites for you!

Index